FOR SUSAN LESLIE

Library of Congress Cataloging-in-Publication Data
Gackenbach, Dick,
Supposes.
"Gulliver books."
Summary: Suppose animals in a variety of situations,
with joking results, such as "Suppose a polar bear had
money. He'd put it in a snow bank!"
1. Animals—Juvenile humor.   2. Wit and humor,
Juvenile.   [1. Animals—Wit and humor.   2. Jokes]
I. Title.
PN6231.A5G34   1989   818'.5402   88-2191
ISBN 0-15-200594-3

Printed in Singapore
First edition A B C D E

The illustrations in this book were done in pen and ink
and Dr. Martin's Radiant Concentrate Water Color
on D'Arches 140-lb. Cold Press Watercolor Paper.
The text type was set in Clearface.
Composition by Thompson Type, San Diego, California
Printed and bound by Tien Wah Press, Singapore
Production supervision by Warren Wallerstein and Ginger Boyer
Designed by Nancy J. Ponichtera

SUPPOSES

by Dick Gackenbach

Gulliver Books

Harcourt Brace Jovanovich

San Diego   New York   London

Suppose a pig painted a fence.

He'd put on three coats!

Suppose a cat ate lemons.

She would turn into a sourpuss!

Suppose snakes had feet.

They would have to buy shoes!

Suppose a hippo went on a diet.

He'd be lean and mean!

Suppose zebras had white stripes.

They do!

Suppose a rabbit was a table.

You would eat a hamburger on a bunny!

Suppose a dormouse was a "d-o-o-r-mouse."

Would the doorknob be a belly button?

Suppose a horse had wings.

He'd be a horsefly!

Suppose giraffes had to wear neckties.

And monkeys would charge a neckle to tie them!

Suppose alligators delivered mail.

Don't send me a letter!

Suppose a polar bear had money.

He'd put it in a snow bank!

Suppose a cow   jumped into your bed.

Better moo over!

Suppose a dinosaur stubbed his toe.

He would be a dino-sore!

And suppose kids had horns for noses.

It would be a toot!